Wendy Baker'

compact
Sketchbook
of accessories

BOOK · COMPANY

157 Watchfield Court, Sutton Court Road, London W4 4NE
Telephone orders: +44 (0) 845 602 1375
email: info@shoestringbooks.co.uk
website: www.shoestringbooks.co.uk

Other books by Wendy Baker:

The Curtain Sketchbook	0-9532939-2-0
The Window and Bed Sketchbook	0-9532939-4-7
Curtain Recipes (hb)	0-9532939-5-5
Curtain Recipes (pb)	0-9549758-0-4
Curtain Recipes (cards)	0-9532939-6-3
Compact Sketchbook of Blinds	0-9532939-8-X
Compact Sketchbook of Accessories	0-9532939-9-8

ILLUSTRATIONS BY CHRISSIE CARRIERE © FOR SHOESTRING BOOK COMPANY

PUBLISHED BY SHOESTRING BOOK COMPANY
© copyright by Wendy Baker 2005

Conceived, edited and designed by Wendy Baker

ISBN   0-9532939-9-8

Printed by Creative Print and Design, London UK
Printed in 2005

WENDY BAKER

introduction...

The compact sketchbook of accessories is filled with ideas showing you how to accessorize your home, whether it is a relaxed country style or a more slick city style that you are trying to achieve. 'Over accessorizing' can sometimes work well but other times it can just look a mess. I personally love 'clutter' but then all of a sudden I feel like throwing everything away and generally clearing the decks. Very minimal accessories can look fantastic - if the one green apple on the plate is correctly placed...but rather like Nouvelle Cuisine it can sometimes look utterly ridicules!

I cannot accessorize your home for you but I have tried to draw from my experience as a designer over the years and imagine your home.....a good starting point is to make sure that your chosen colours are right - experiment with mini pots of paint, dab various colours of paint on your walls and live with them for a while before you commit to an expensive repaint. Check that your furniture is in the best position to allow you to walk around the room easily, see that you can look at the view if there is one and most important of all that you are comfortable when you are in the room. Then it comes to the best part I think...the accessories!

This is not as easy as it seems.... for instance a beautiful vase, with the simplest of flowers and the right light can be all you need to give a finishing touch to a certain corner - it makes the right statement and you don't have to go any further..and then another time that vase looks wrong and perhaps needs other accessories to show it off - it's just a matter of having the right balance. By contrast I found when I lived in the country that I liked to have more clutter around me - like a comforter - I wanted to be cocooned more - don't ask me why...

I hope you enjoy some of my ideas..and that you find them not only helpful but that it will teach you to change the way you place your ornaments, cushions or collectables - when you manage to create that certain coziness to a family room or the right kind of elegance to a formal living room just by adding the right accessory in the right place then you are well on your way.

contents...

choosing your style...

There really are no hard and fast rules nowadays when choosing a style for your home. Gone are the days when, if you lived in a period house, you had matching period furniture and consequently matching period accessories! Now we tend to have a mixture of styles all together in one room. It's great fun just buying bits and pieces here and there, things that take your fancy, but it's often when you get them back home that you realise that perhaps you have gone slightly over the top - then you have to decide to live with it, move it to another room or take it back!

When you start to accessorize a room try to make a sort of cameo picture - group things together - nothing looks more boring than say a small picture in the middle of a wall and at the wrong height - get all the pictures together for that room and put them into a nice pattern (I do this on the floor to make sure it looks right before banging holes in the walls!) - I have given you lots of examples of how to do this in the book. Of course it's the way I like to do things - it may not be your way but it will perhaps help to create your own look - something that you feel comfortable living with..

getting the colours right...

I'm a great believer in choosing neutral colours for your basic walls, at least to start with anyway. I live in France and my house faces South and is therefore bright, I have used 4 different shades of 'white'and it works really well. You can always be more adventurous once you have started to add your accessories then you may want to add a colour on one wall to add some warmth to a dark corner or to emphasize a particular item.

fabric and trimming selection...

Mix prints, checks, stripes or two tone plain fabrics
together – try experimenting with different tones
of fabrics as well as different textures – take into
account the wall coverings and the curtains and
keep the accessories simple and to the point - once
you have decided on your scheme stick to it, don't
keep adding more and more different colours as all
that will do is to end up looking a mess.
If you decide on two tone on tone fabrics for your
cushions add some trimmings in a mixture of the
two colours – most fabric manufacturers also have
trimming ranges to tie in with their fabrics and it
adds a finishing touch to the accessory...

fabric and trimming selection...

1
2
3
4
5
6
7
8
9
10
11
12
13

fabric and trimming selection...

1

2

3

4

5

6

7

8

9

10

11

12

1

2

3

5

4

6

7

8

9

10

11

12

fabric and trimming selection...

- deep tones of red

12

1

2

fabric and trimming selection...

- strong greens and pinks

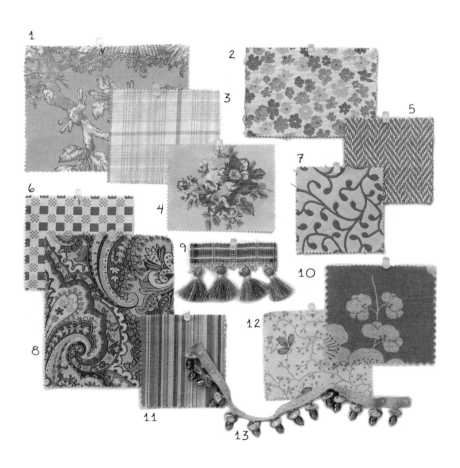

fabric and trimming selection...

- neutrals with a touch of soft blues

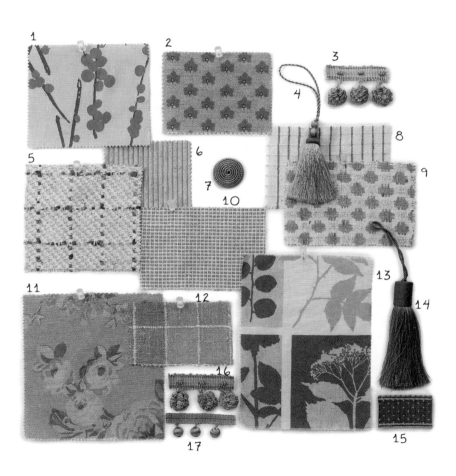

1
2
3
4
5
6
7
8
9
10
11
12
13
14
15
16
17

using chairs as an accessory...

- chairs are not just for sitting on!

chairs as an accessory...

- paint a few odd chairs different colours and transform them

make a reading corner...

making a statement...

- a stunning black and white print on the chairs and striped footstools

a selection of upholstered chairs...

- using bold colourful fabrics

button backed armchairs...

- 'dress' tall windows with a matching pair of armchairs

modern armchair...

armchair...

- simple modern lines for the chair and an old
fashioned rose print for the cover

I LIKE TO MIX 'GRANNY' PRINTS WITH SIMPLE MODERN
STYLE FURNITURE — IT WORKS REALLY WELL...

a classic modern design...

- in white leather

- NOT VERY PRACTABLE BUT A WONDERFUL LUXURY!

modern lounger...

- make this the only colour in the room – it will look stunning

and after...

- with the armchairs completing the picture

occasional tables...

add a table...

- a well placed candelabra highlights these curtains beautifully

create an interesting corner...

- a tall vase and flowers will add height to the corner

a solid piece of wood...

- used as a table

brilliant red perspex coffee table...

- add various other accessories in the same strong colour

a carved stone based table...

- only works if the hall is square and large

PAINT AN OLD METAL TABLE ONE OF THE
COLOURS IN THE RUG TO GIVE IT NEW LIFE...

working with pictures...

- and mirrors

IT'S VERY IMPORTANT TO GROUP YOUR PICTURES AND
MIRRORS TOGETHER AS IT MAKES MORE OF AN IMPACT...

working with pictures...

- three paintings in identical frames make more of a statement when hung like this

a mixture of pictures and mirrors...

- adding a standard lamp helps to bring a corner of a room alive

hallways are very important...

- pictures look best when evenly spaced as below

big mirrors for big rooms...

- if you are lucky enough to have an enormous mirror like this, then show it off by making it the centre of attraction!

place two black mirrors side by side...

- looks great

pictures and photographs...

pictures on the floor...

- if you have a stunning wallpaper like this why spoil it!

A BEAUTIFUL
CARVED MIRROR
LIKE THIS SHOULD
BE SHOWN OFF OVER
THE MANTELPIECE

pictures of different sizes...

an hallway before...

trimmings for lampshades...

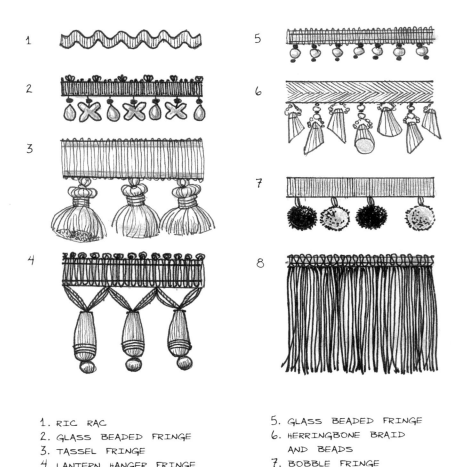

1. RIC RAC
2. GLASS BEADED FRINGE
3. TASSEL FRINGE
4. LANTERN HANGER FRINGE

5. GLASS BEADED FRINGE
6. HERRINGBONE BRAID
   AND BEADS
7. BOBBLE FRINGE
8. CUT FRINGE

lampshades...

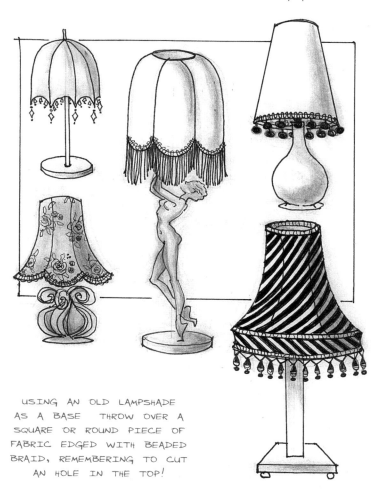

USING AN OLD LAMPSHADE
AS A BASE   THROW OVER A
SQUARE OR ROUND PIECE OF
FABRIC EDGED WITH BEADED
BRAID, REMEMBERING TO CUT
AN HOLE IN THE TOP!

basic shapes...

1. EMPIRE
2. COOLIE
3. CYLINDER
4. CONE

5. DRUM
6. RECTANGLE
7. SQUARE EMPIRE

LAMPSHADES CAN BE MADE IN
ANY FABRIC — SOMETIMES THE
BOLDER THE BETTER!
...OR KEEP IT SIMPLE AND MATCH
THE LAMPSHADE TO THE BASE

wall lights....uplighters...

- it's essential to put wall lights on a dimmer switch

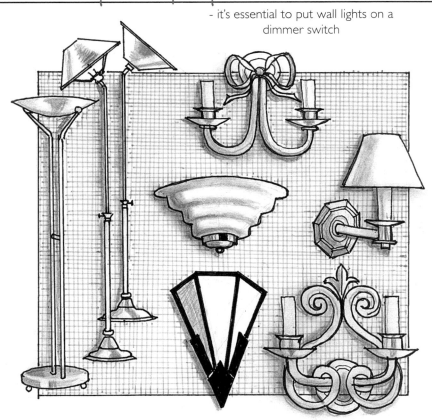

UPLIGHTERS ADD HEIGHT TO THE ROOM. I OFTEN
USE A FLOOR OR TABLE MOUNTED SPOTLIGHT DIRECTED
AT SAY SOME FLOWERS OR AN IMPORTANT STATUE AND HAVE
THIS ON A SEPARATE SWITCH SO THAT WHEN YOU COME
INTO THE ROOM THE FIRST LIGHT YOU SWITCH ON IS
SHINING AT THAT PARTICULAR FEATURE

desk lamps...

I LOVE THE LITTLE 'PEBBLE' LIGHT AND THE CUBE AND
GIVE THEM TO ALL MY FRIENDS AS PRESENTS...I TELL
THEM TO LEAVE ONE ON ALWAYS SOMEWHERE IN THE HOUSE
24 HOURS A DAY IT WORKS   AS A COMFORTER — OR A
NIGHTLIGHT FOR CHILDREN.

hanging lights...

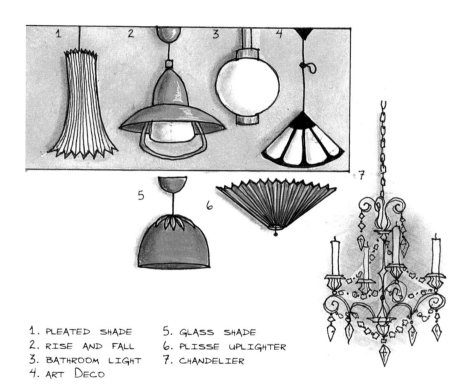

1. PLEATED SHADE
2. RISE AND FALL
3. BATHROOM LIGHT
4. ART DECO

5. GLASS SHADE
6. PLISSE UPLIGHTER
7. CHANDELIER

standard lamps...

- or does one call them just' freestanding lamps' these days?

57

balanced lighting...

THE TWO TABLE LIGHTS SHOULD BE ON DIMMERS AND SO SHOULD
THE PICTURE LIGHT. ALSO HAVE   SEPARATE SWITCHES AS you MAY
NOT ALWAYS WANT ALL THE LIGHTS ON AT THE SAME TIME

table lighting...

- make sure the lights shine on the table not into
your eyes —again put them on dimmer switches

screens...

- use them for screening off a washing area

THE FABRIC IS TIED ONTO THE SCREEN WHICH MAKES IT EASY FOR WASHING AWAY THOSE STICKY FINGER MARKS BUT IS ALSO IDEAL SHOULD YOU WANT TO CHANGE THE FABRIC AS YOUR CHILD GROWS UP...

- with a sprinkling of stars

oriental style screen...

- this screen would be perfect to have made in a translucent fabric either to allow the light in from a window or it could be illuminated from behind by a small floor spot.

adaptable screens...

- use instead of curtains especially for very tall windows

screens - a million and one uses...

- this particular screen is being used as dressing room — nowadays many people have their bathrooms and bedrooms as one and this idea gives a little privacy.

useful screens...

art deco screen...

- use as wardrobe doors

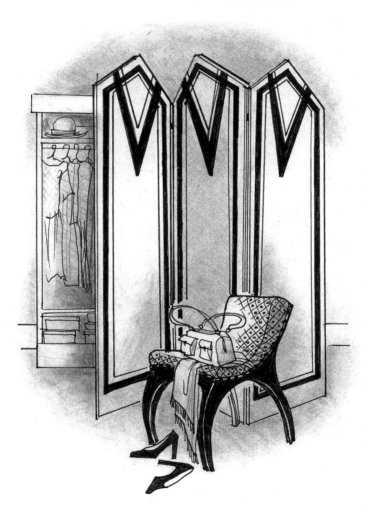

damask screen...

THIS WAY YOU CAN SEE THE FULL
RICHNESS OF THE FABRIC

basic cushion shapes...

- use feather filling not synthetic rubbish!

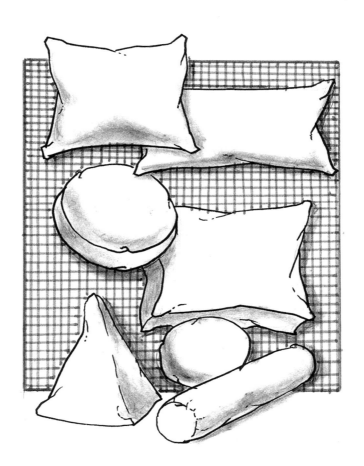

trimmings for cushions...

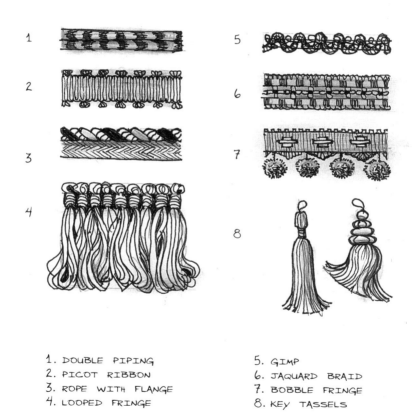

1. DOUBLE PIPING
2. PICOT RIBBON
3. ROPE WITH FLANGE
4. LOOPED FRINGE

5. GIMP
6. JAQUARD BRAID
7. BOBBLE FRINGE
8. KEY TASSELS

THIS IS ONE OF THE TIMES THAT
I THINK YOU SHOULD PILE ON THE
CUSHIONS — MIX PRINTS WITH
CHECKS AND STRIPES...PLENTY OF
TRIMMINGS TOO

- experiment with some black Russia braid and
make your own pattern to tie in with the decor

two toned cushions...

- choose two colours that compliment each other...

THE TWO MATTRESS CUSHIONS HAVE TICKING
INSETS WHICH ALWAYS LOOKS NICE AND COMES
IN SEVERAL COLOURS... AND THE 'POODLE' CUSHION
IS MY DOG BEATRICE'S FAVOURITE TOY!

silk cushions...

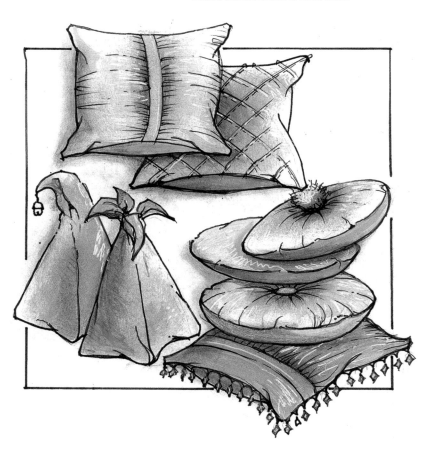

USE DELICATE COLOURS FOR THESE RUCHED AND PIN
TUCKED CUSHIONS — TRIM WITH BEADS AND POM POMS
— AND THE OCCASIONAL BELL!

country cushions...

- a mixture of shapes and patterns

THIS IS A GOOD TIME TO USE UP ODD
BITS AND PIECES OF LEFT OVER FABRICS
- AND IT LOOKS LESS CONTRIVED

stools...

- useful as extra seating

throws...

- use two or three throws on a sofa ...

IT ALWAYS SEEMS SILLY TO HAVE THESE THROWN
OVER THE ARM OF A SOFA OR CHAIR AND NEVER USED
- PERSONALLY IF YOU ARE GOING TO BUY OR MAKE
SOMETHING I THINK YOU SHOULD USE IT!

- checks, prints and textures

TRY PUTTING A THICK WOOL 'BLANKET
STITCH' AROUND THE EDGE AND A KNITTED
BACK ON TO A CUSHION

make a comfortable corner...

- and a pretty picture too

comfortable sofa...

- cover your sofa with a big rug or two and then pile
on some cushions ...always looks very inviting...

strong colours...

- my favourite colour combination...

I CAN IMAGINE THESE CUSHIONS, EXACTLY
AS THEY ARE IN THE PICTURE, ON A GINGER
COLOURED SOFA — PERFECT!

take an empty room...

BEFORE YOU CLUTTER THE ROOM WITH FURNITURE HAVE A
LONG LOOK AT WHAT THE ROOM HAS TO 'SAY' — THIS
ONE HAS LOW BEAMED CEILINGS BUT PLENTY OF LIGHT —
SO TRY TO ACCESSORIZE TO SUIT THE ROOM. KEEP THE
FURNITURE TO A MINIMUM DON'T OVER POWER THE ROOM.
DRESS THE SOFA WITH BLACK AND WHITE CUSHIONS,
NOT TOO MANY. POLISH THE FLOOR BOARDS AND ADD A
RUG — THIS GIVES A SENSE OF SPACE.

add a few accessories...

- just to complete the picture...

- create your own style

HERE I'VE JUST USED BLACK AND WHITE AND IT ALWAYS WORKS!

kitchen style...

- again black and white accessories but this time I used
Art Deco china and clock

- LET THE CHINA DICTATE THE COLOUR OF THE KITCHEN

modern kitchen...

- before accessorizing

transformation...

- with some carefully placed fruit to add a splash
of colour to a stainless steel kitchen

kitchen clutter...

- I just love bits and pieces hanging on lines or stuffed into jars

YOU CAN TELL A LOT FROM A PERSON'S CLUTTER
AND THE MORE CRAMMED EVERYTHING IS THE MORE
INTERESTING IT IS!

my 'clutter'...

- I live in France and my kitchen is very 'Provencal' - but the
lighting is simple and modern

- compliment with striped china and fabrics...

...and a pink AGA...

- there are so many fabulous colours to choose from but pink is great fun!

A SCRUBBED PINE PLATE RACK, ANTIQUE WOULD LOOK
BEST, GIVES A DEAD CORNER A BIT OF CHARACTER

kitchen rugs...

— BUY AN ANTIQUE RUG FROM THE
SALEROOMS AND TRANSFORM YOUR KITCHEN
— AVOID COOKING AREAS!

welsh dressers...

- brightly coloured walls...and an abundance of pretty pink china

kitchen shelves...

THESE BRACKETS ARE OLD CAST IRON ONES I
BOUGHT IN A MARKET BUT THERE ARE SOME FANTASTIC
COPIES AROUND — GO TO AN OLD FASHIONED
IRONMONGERS — IF YOU CAN FIND ONE!

dressing up a window...

- with dried hops or bunches of dried wild flowers

in this kitchen corner...

- find an old column and put some nice green Ivy on top

- IT LOOKS SO FRESH ESPECIALLY IF
  YOUR KITCHEN IS VERY PLAIN

- a breakfast tray

- would look nice with a pink AGA?

borders on rugs...

- there are some exciting borders to add to a basic carpet
around and many carpet manufacturers now do special
orders with your own colour combinations...

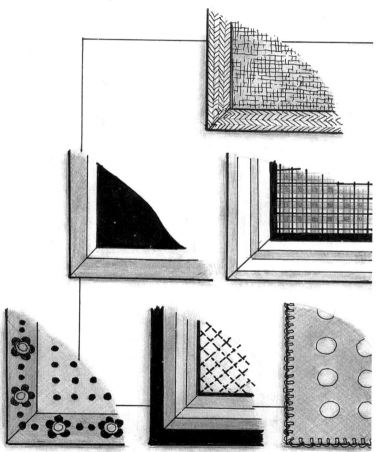

- this rug can be made in other amazing colours...

children's rugs...

bedside rug...

– YOU NEED A RUG
BESIDE THE BED,
ESPECIALLY IF YOU HAVE
WOODEN FLOORS...

an old rug in the kitchen...

- I like this look for a kitchen it's very comforting...

a really colourful patchwork rug...

- in a country hall

- IT REMINDS ME OF COLD DAYS AND LOG FIRES...

black and greys mixed...

- is a really nice combination for a rug

this dramatic rug is just the best!...

- you don't really need anything else in the room...

various shapes and sizes of vases...

- I collect vases so there are too many to show but these are a few that I use the most at the moment...

VASES ARE BECOMING MORE FLAMBOYANT AND IMPORTANT... WELL IT'S A FAD I SUPPOSE BUT I THINK IT'S QUITE NICE...EVERYONE LIKES FLOWERS BUT DON'T OVERDO IT, OFTEN THE SIMPLEST OF ARRANGEMENTS LOOKS BEST...

wonderful red Poppies...

a jardinière with hydrangeas...

- make a picture by grouping pieces of furniture together

my lovely cream pot...

- just two lilies but it works so well in my hall in France...

yellow daffodils...

- THE BLIND LOOKS GOOD WITH THE
FLOWERS AND AGAIN THE GROUPING MAKES A
INTERESTING PICTURE...

a 'stick' table...

- shown here with a very wide striped
wallpaper and matching flowers...

a metal shelf with an orchid...

- in a tin vase - this useful shelf works
well in a cloakroomor in a hallway...

delicate blossoms in a glass vase...

- don't be tempted to put more than
this in the vase...

just a simple white vase...

- filled with renunculas to match the wallpaper!

a simple pure white bathroom...

- and just three anemones...

collectables...

- hats and walking sticks are the most common collected items...

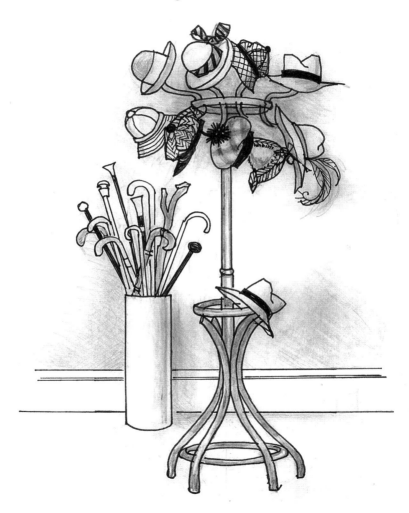

New England birds...

- or are they 'Shaker' birds? They are such lovely shapes...

collectable dolls...

a collection of 1920's shoes...

- in fabulous shapes and colours

WHETHER THEY ARE BLACK OR
WHITE AND AS LONG AS THEY
DON'T HAVE BIRDS IN THEM!

scent bottles...

FRENCH MARKETS ARE
FILLED WITH THESE –
AND AS THEY ARE VERY
SORT AFTER THEY TEND
TO BE EXPENSIVE...

fabric covered hat boxes...

- smaller ones were used for keeping trinkets in...

starched white linen...

- or antique printed floral linen - displayed in an Armoire

- some of my jugs are quite delicate and the patterns are partially worn away but they are still precious to me...

- not so much now but that is possibly because we
have killed off most of the beautiful butterflies!

- but in a burnt orange with striped
Directors chairs

moorish umbrellas...

- they can be found in wonderful colours
  and with tassels and beads and bells....

decking an outside area...

- is still very fashionable and it works well in the city

HANG SOME COLOURFUL LANTERNS AROUND FOR FUN...

wooden 'lovers' seat...

- surrounded by Box trees in modern slate coloured pots

- eating outdoors is everyone's favourite

- sitting in the shade...

PRETTY FLOWERED TABLE RUNNER

metal furniture...

- is very popular

DON'T BE TEMPTED
TO PAINT THE FURNITURE
ETC, LEAVE IT OUTSIDE
AND IT WILL WEATHER
BEAUTIFULLY...

metal arbour...

a picnic at the seaside...

- treat yourself to a hamper basket

THERE IS NOTHING LIKE LUNCH ON THE BEACH!

table linen...

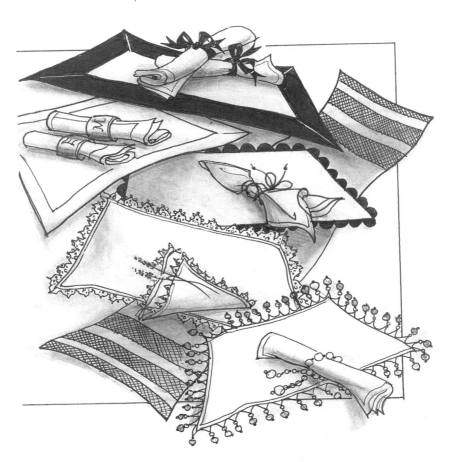

NAPKIN RINGS CAN BE MADE FROM ANYTHING — I USE STRING,
RIBBONS OR BEADS DEPENDING ON THE TABLE SETTING ...

formal table setting...

- try adding a band of contrast fabric to match the china . . .

a wonderful hand painted screen...

- makes a perfect setting for a romantic dinner

dinner for two...

- in candlelight on the patio

exciting patterned plates...

- there are so many wonderful patterns to
choose from at the moment

USE PLAIN TABLE LINEN TO 'SHOW OFF'
THE ELABORATE CHINA PATTERNS

family breakfast table...

- striped runners work really well on a wooden table
and are easier to wash than a big tablecloth...

check tablecloth...

- can be coated for kitchen use

antique markets...

What to look for . . .

Tea towels (Les Tourchons) appeared first in the 13th century - crisp and simple, off white with red initials modestly cross-stitched in the corner. In the 19th century girls would embroider their own initials in the corner and when they were getting married they would add their finaces initials beside theirs!

Provencial fabrics (les Indiennes) electric coloured prints originally made in India, hand blocked and coloured with vegetable dye. They became very popular in the 60s and 70s copied by Souleido. who revived them but now perhaps a little passe.

Linens (le linge) white or off white - beautifully embroidered and edged with intricate laces. Very collectable - look for tea towels, pillow cases and table cloths - all can be adapted into window coverings PURE MAGIC...

Most markets have plenty of cutlery and napkin rings but be careful not to pay over the odds for silver, take a silver hallmark book with you to check the markings If you are spending a lot of money I think I would feel safer going to antique shop rather than a stall...unless you know what you are doing of course!

Where to Go . . .

If you live in France, as I do, you will find every little village has its own market day. Here are a few that I know:

Nice - every Monday big antique market - very good
Val bonne - 1st Sunday in every month - 3 very good linen stalls
St Tropez - every Saturday large market worth a visit
Antibes - Saturday mornings
Aix-en-Provence - Saturdays are best - worth a visit
L'Isle-sur-Sorge - Sundays - wonderful tiles too
Cannes - 1st Sunday of each month
Paris - Puces de St Ouen (porte de Clignancourt) wonderful flea market Saturday, Sunday and Monday.

antique markets...

UK MARKETS AND SHOPS

Alfie's Antique Market
020 7723 6066

Grays' Antique Market
02076297034

Guinevere Antiques
020 7736 29 17

Lunn Antiques
020 7736 4638 -
lunnantiqueS@aol.com

Dierdre's Shop -
Talbot Walk - Ripley; Surrey

Tobias & the Angel -
White Hart Lane,
London, SW 1 3

Portobello Market -
Portobello Road, London W 1 1
- Saturdays best

Kempton Race Course Market
-Sunbury, Surrey -
2nd & last Tuesday each month
01932 782 292

Sandown Racecourse market
Esher. Surrey -
0171 249 4050

Lasco architectural salvage

Walcot Reclamation

The 3 below are sponsored by
the Daily Mail. For details call
01636702 326

Ardingly - Sussex.
NewarkLincolnshire.
MalvernWorcestershire

fabric and trimmings...

On the following pages I have listed the fabric
and trimming manufacturers names and
reference numbers - contact them for your
nearest stockists if you are not a trade buyer.

fabric and trimmings...

- details for fabrics on page 9

1. Mulberry – Grenadine FD235 A117
2. Lewis and Wood – Jazz black LW 108106
3. Designers Guild - F1162/03
4. Kravet -16267 col 18
5. Zimmer & Rohde - Jazz 18 10039 984
6. Robert Allen – Waynesburg black
7. Robert Allen - Wigginton black
8. Osborne & Little -Dusa F5444-04
9. Robert & Allen – checker square black
10. Lee Jofa -202194 Bills plaid col 8
11. Osborne & Little - Picot Braid T525/04
12. Osborne & Little narrow picot braid T524/04

fabric and trimmings...

- details for fabrics on page 10

1. Anna French – bird in the bush col 21
2. Ralph Lauren – FLFY 25030 Fenwick Aisle floral/indigo
3. Ralph Lauren - FLFY 23905 Great Point Gingham /indigo
4. G.P.J. Baker J0501 Oriel col 650
5. Zimmer & Rohde – 10080 – 593
6. Kravet – 25751 5 Exclusive
7. Noblis – Weekend 39006
8. Donghia – Vinaya col 02
9. Wendy Cushing Passementerie - double tassel fringe
10. Kravet – 25746 col 5
11. Mulberry – FD 159/667 Rhode Island Roses Col H101
12. Zoffany - Flower braid TRM07004

fabric and trimmings...

- details for fabrics on page 11

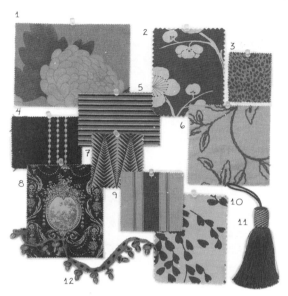

1. Osborne & Little – Wild Chrysanthemum – F5440/01
2. Romo – 7185/06 Cardamon
3. Kravet – Ellis – 616
4. Malabar – Patta 01
5. Manuel Canovas – Lucca 4568/06
6. Sheila Coombes – Summer Palace – Tatiana 01
7. Neisha Crosland – small Zebra pigment/ brown string
8. Robert Allen – Versailles – black
9. Knowles & Christou - one ply
10. Romo – 7816/06 Sapporo Cardamon
11. Wendy Cushing Passementerie - braided tassel
12. Nina Campbell - Lantern fringe

fabric and trimmings...

- details for fabrics on page 12

1. Manuel Canovas – La Promenade 1488/03
2. Lee Jofa – 2430 GWF La Florentina col 97
3. Manuel Canovas Bernice – Cardinal 4519/15
4. Manuel Canovas Misia 01486/01
5. Wendy Cushing Passementerie - raspberry fringe
6. William Yoeward – FW032/01
7. Lee Jofa - 2408 GWF Waterfall stripe col 687
8. Malabar – Chinois
9. Wendy Cushing Passementerie – cut fringe with hangers

fabric and trimmings...

- details for fabrics on page 13

1. Mulberry Patchwork
2. Zoffany - TRM0/9002

fabric and trimmings...

- details for fabrics on page 14

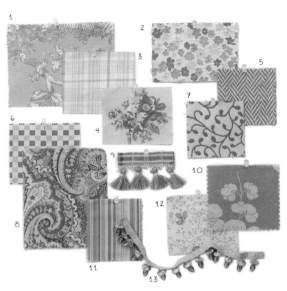

1. Kravet – Ballard col 23
2. Liberty – Mosetta Mimi LF L 350/04
3. Robert Allen – Rothchild col Flamingo
4. Elanbach – Uzes Scatter – green
5. Salamandre 26662 – 001
6. Elanbach - chequers green /brown
7. Salamandre – 26664/001
8. Lee Jofa 2004091/37
9. Kravet - tassel braid
10. Romo – chidori Kiwi 7185/02
11. Mulberry – Portofino stripe FD521J116
12. Elanbach – Vasily trail/green
13. Nina Campbell - lantern fringe

fabric and trimmings...

- details for fabrics on page 15

1.	Knowles and Christou - ' Sticks' pattern on silk	
2.	Elanbach - maple/brown	
3.	Kravet - pom pom fringe	
4.	Wemyss Houles – Lolita 35191 col 9680	
5..	Brain Yates Silkana – Silksin 1110003-02	
6.	Designers Guild F1212/01 linen	
7.	Kravet – button	
8.	Malabar – Indian silk – NSIL-12	
9.	Malabar – Indian silk	
10.	Malabar – Indian silk – NSIL – 19	

11. Anna French –
    Birds in the bush col 71
12. Beacon Hill – Tendail
    plaid/carmel mist
13. Osborne & Little –
    Boheme/F5446/01
14. Wemyss Houles –
    Kabuk 35206 -9900
15. Kravet Polka dot T30304/615
16. Kravet - pom pom fringe
17. Kravet - satin beaded freing

U.K. suppliers list...

FABRICS

ANNA FRENCH

ANDREW MARTIN

BERY DESIGNS

BRIAN YATES

BRUNSCHWIG & FILS

CATH KIDSTON

CABBAGES & ROSES

CHASE ERWIN

COLEFAX & FOWLER

DESIGNERS GUILD

DONGHIA

ELANBACH

G.P. & J. BAKER

JANE CHURCHILL

JOHN LEWIS (retail)

KA INTERNATIONAL (retail)
Interior stores' world wide

KNOWLES & CHRISTOU

KRAVET

LAURA ASHLEY (RETAIL)

LEE JOFA

NEISHA CROSLAND

OSBORNE AND LITTLE

PONGEES

ROMO

ROBERT ALLEN

SALAMANDRE

TURNELL & GIGON
(SCHUMACHER & GREEF)

LEWIS & WOOD

ZIMMER & ROHDE

ZOFFANY

U.K. suppliers list...

TRIMMINGS (PASSEMENTERIE)

BRITISH TRIMMINGS

CASTELLANO-BELTRAME

COLEFAX AND FOWLER

HENRY NEWBERY

JANE CHURCHILL

OSBORNE AND LITTLE

PRICE AND COMPANY

V.V. ROULEAUX

WENDY CUSHING
PASSEMENTERIE

WEMMYS HOULES

LIGHTING

BESSELINK & JONES

BELLA FIGURA

CHRISTOPHER WRAY

EMILY TODHUNTER

HABITAT (retail)

HEALS (retail)

PORTA ROMANA

NOHO (retail)

VAUGHAN

CHINA & GLASS

BRIDGEWATER

CATH KIDSTON

CONRAN (retail)

DESIGNERS'GUILD

DIVERTIMENTI (retail)

GENERAL TRADING COMPANY
(retail)

HABITAT (retail)

HEALS (retail)

U.K. suppliers list...

JOHN LEWIS (retail)

NINA CAMPBELL

SKANDUIM (retail)

WILLIAM YOEWARD

SUMMERILL & BISHOP

GARDEN FURNITURE

LINDSEY

MARSTON & LANGINGER

RUGS

THE RUG COMPANY

CONRAN (retail)

CATH KIDSTON

HILL & COMPANY

FLOWERS & VASES

ABSOLUTE FLOWERS

PULBROOK & GOULD

MOYSES STEVENS

WOODHAMS

MIRRORS

GRAHAM & GREEN

ON REFLECTION

LASCO ARCHETECTURAL

WALCOT RECLAIMATION

LINENS
(Remember most stores have good linen departments)

ANTIQUE DESIGNS (trade)

COLOGNE & COTTON

DESIGNERS' GUILD

THE WHITE COMPANY

VOLGA (Trade & retail)

LUNNS ANTIQUES

U.K. suppliers list...

CHAIRS

ANDREW MARTIN

CONRAN

HEALS

THE DINING CHAIR COMPANY

GEORGE SMITH

TABLES

INTER DESIGN (trade)

KNOWLES & CHRISTOU (glass)

NINA CAMPBELL

NOHO (glass)

LININGS/WORKROOM SUNDRIES

COPE AND TIMMINS

EDMUND BELL

JONES INTERIORS

JOHN LEWIS RETAIL BRANCHES THROUGHOUT U.K.

McCULLOCH AND WALLIS (retail)

PRETTY FRILLS

PRICE AND COMPANY

RUFFLETTE

STREETS

SHOWROOMS TO VISIT

CHELSEA HARBOUR DESIGN CENTRE
020 7225 9 149
enquirieS@chelsea-harbour.co.uk

ASSOCIATIONS

BIDA (BRITISH INTERIOR DESIGN ASSOCIATION)
020 7349 0800
enquirieS@bida.ory

U.S. suppliers list...

FABRIC MANUFACTURERS TO LOOK FOR...

(Many fabric houses can be seen at the various d&d centers)

ANNA FRENCH
BEACON HILL
ANDREW MARTIN
BRAIN YATES
BRUNSCHWIG & FILS
CHASE ERWIN
COLEFAX & FOWLER
DESIGNERS' GUILD
DONGHIA
G.P.J.BAKER
JANE CHURCHILL
HOLLY HUNT
KRAVET
LEE JOFA
NINA CAMPBELL
OSBORNE & LITTLE
ROMO
ROBERT ALLEN
SCHUMACHER
WAVERLEY
WESCO
ZIMMER & ROHDE
ZOFFANY

PASSEMENTERIE/TRIMMINGS

SAMUEL AND SONS
HOULES
KRAVET

CHINA/GLASS/LINEN/CUSHIONS

ABC CARPET & HOME
ANTHROPOLIGIE
CRATE & BARREL
POTTERY BARN
GRACIOUS HOMES
DEPARTMENT STORES...

RUGS

ABC CARPET AND HOME
THE RUG COMPANY
MOST DEPARTMENT STORES...

WORKROOM SUPPLIERS ETC...

BECKENSTIEN HOME
HAYNES (LININGS)

FURNITURE IN GENERAL

ANTIQUE MARKETS OR STORES AND DESIGN CENTERS...

HERE ARE A FEW DESIGN CENTERS...

D & D BUILDING – NEW YORK
PEACHTREE HILL AVENUE – ATLANTA
PACIFIC DESIGN CENTRE – WEST HOLLYWOOD
DESIGN CENTER – DALLAS
DESIGN CENTER – BOSTON
DESIGN CENTER – SAN FRANSISCO

DEPARTMENT STORES

(With good home departments)

ABC CARPET AND HOME
BARNEY'S
BED BATH AND BEYOND
BLOOMINGDALES
MACY'S
TAKASHIMAYA